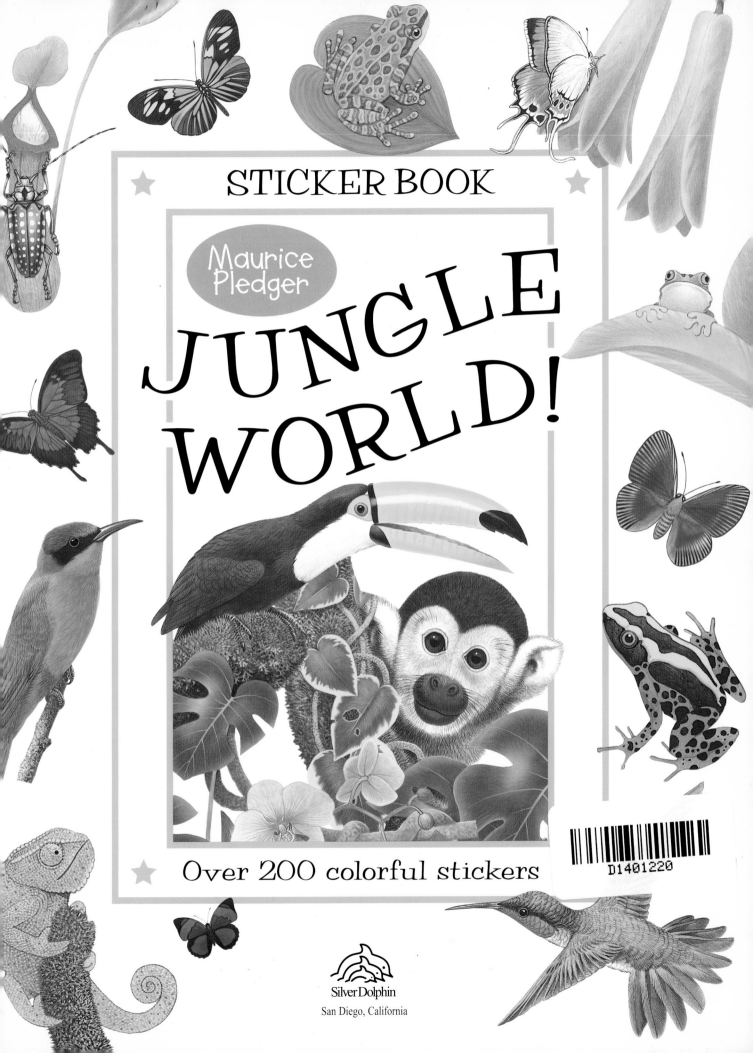

STICKER BOOK

Maurice Pledger

JUNGLE WORLD!

Over 200 colorful stickers

Silver Dolphin
San Diego, California

D1401220

Silver Dolphin

Silver Dolphin Books

An imprint of the Advantage Publishers Group
5880 Oberlin Drive, San Diego, CA 92121-4794
www.silverdolphinbooks.com

Illustration copyright © 2003 by Maurice Pledger/Bernard Thornton Agency, London

Text and design copyright © 2003 by The Templar Company plc

ISBN 1-59223-221-3

Designed by Caroline Reeves
Edited by Beth Harwood and A.J. Wood

Made in Italy

2 3 4 5 6   08 07 06 05 04

About this book

In this book you can join Tavi Tiger and her animal friends and learn all about the many different creatures that live in jungles all over the world.

Turn to the back of the book and you'll find lots of stickers, too. Use them to complete the sticker activities on every page by filling in the animal shapes or by making your own jungle pictures.

Have fun as you explore the world of the jungle!

What's in the jungle?

Jungles, often called rain forests, are full of amazing creatures. There are animals of almost every kind— furry creatures like Tavi Tiger, beautiful birds, lots of incredible insects, and more.

In fact, jungles are home to more living things than any other place on earth! Look for all the different types of animals as you go on your journey through the jungle.

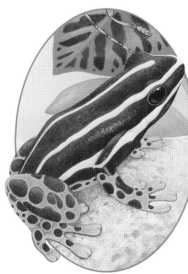

Peter
Parakeet

Benny
Bush Baby

Frida Frog

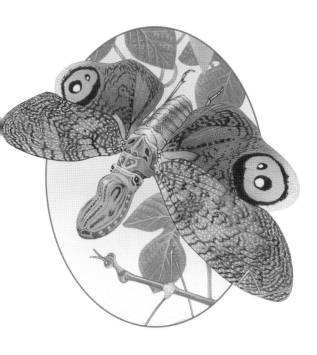

Bethany Bug

Ollie Ocelot

Carla Chameleon

Emma
Egret

Here are some of Tavi's favorite friends. Fill in their pictures with your stickers as you meet them in the book.

In the treetops

Welcome to Peter Parakeet's treetop home.
Apart from his jungle-floor friends like Tavi,
most of Peter's friends are good at flying!
Many are birds, like this toucan, or brightly
colored jungle insects. But did you know
that some mammals can fly, too? The flying
squirrel uses flaps under his arms as wings
so he can glide from tree to tree. Find
a sticker of a flying squirrel to add
to this picture, as well as
three more of Peter's
flying friends!

Jungle birds

There are hundreds of different jungle birds. Many are brightly colored and some look very strange, with their big beaks and fantastic feathers. Here are some of Peter Parakeet's beautiful bird friends. Fill in their pictures with the right stickers from your sticker sheet. Which one do you think has the biggest, brightest beak?

Splendid blue wren

Toucan

Cockatoo

Bee-eater

Hummingbirds

Bird of
paradise

Parrot

Cotinga

Rhinoceros
hornbill

Paradise birds

These beautiful birds of paradise live in the rain forests of Papua New Guinea, which is in Southeast Asia. The male birds like to show off their bright colors and pretty feathers to impress the females. Some birds even perform dances or make fancy nests to prove they are the best! Some of these birds like to eat insects. Add three colorful beetle stickers to the picture for them to catch.

Did you know that the hummingbird is the smallest bird in the world? Find the right sticker to fill in this picture of a hummingbird.

Among the branches

Just below the treetops is a vast tangle of branches stretching for miles above the jungle floor. This is where Benny Bush Baby lives, along with other furry creatures such as this squirrel monkey and loris. But there are other types of creatures living here, too. Use your stickers to add a tree shrew, a brightly colored tree frog, and a lizard to the picture.

13

Climbing creatures

Many of Benny Bush Baby's tree-dwelling friends spend so much time climbing among the jungle branches that they never touch the jungle floor! Fill in their sticker shapes, then turn the page and make your own picture of life in the jungle treetops.

Squirrel monkey

Tree shrew

Aye-aye

Sloth

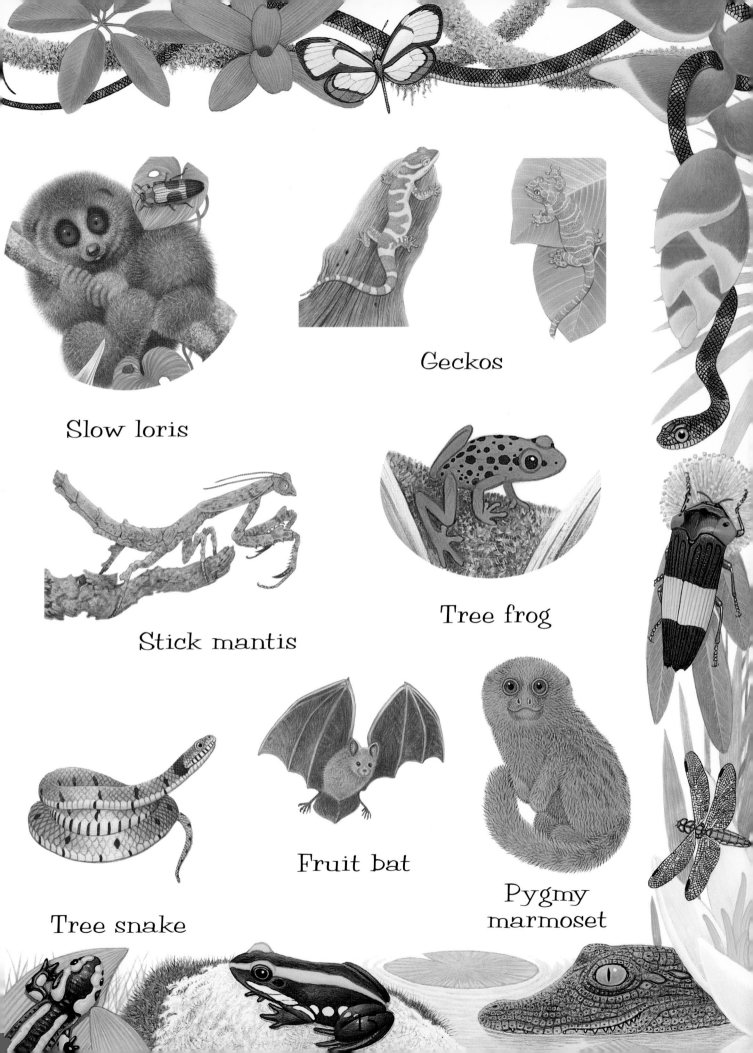

Slow loris

Geckos

Stick mantis

Tree frog

Tree snake

Fruit bat

Pygmy
marmoset

On the jungle floor

Tavi Tiger has lots of other friends who live among the wonderful plants that grow on the floor of the jungle. It's a great place for a game of hide-and-seek! Can you spot Ollie Ocelot hiding somewhere? Now find a sticker to add Tavi's friend Molly Mouse to this scene.

Look for three more of Tavi's friends who live in this part of the jungle. Match your stickers to their pictures below.

Carla Chameleon

Bethany Bug

Frida Frog

Colorful chameleons

Carla Chameleon and her relatives are part of a big family of animals called reptiles. They are great at hiding because they can change color to match their surroundings! This helps them catch nice, juicy insects to eat. Use your stickers to add five insects to the picture for them to creep up on!

Use your stickers to fill in these pictures of four other types of reptiles.

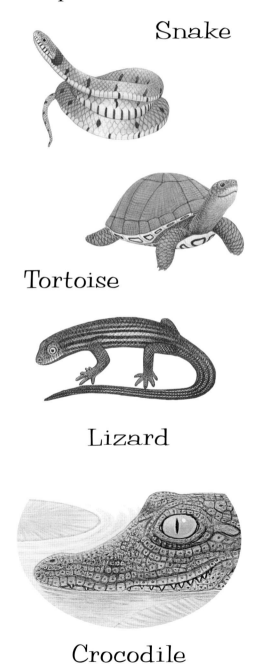

Snake

Tortoise

Lizard

Crocodile

⭐ Lizards and snakes

Of all the reptiles in the jungle, Tavi likes the geckos best. Geckos are a kind of lizard and they have special sticky toes that help them cling onto smooth things like rocks! But not all jungle reptiles are so friendly. When she's out and about, Tavi always

keeps an eye out for snakes. There are lots of different types and though some are harmless, many have a poisonous bite. Now use your stickers to fill in these pictures of some jungle reptiles.

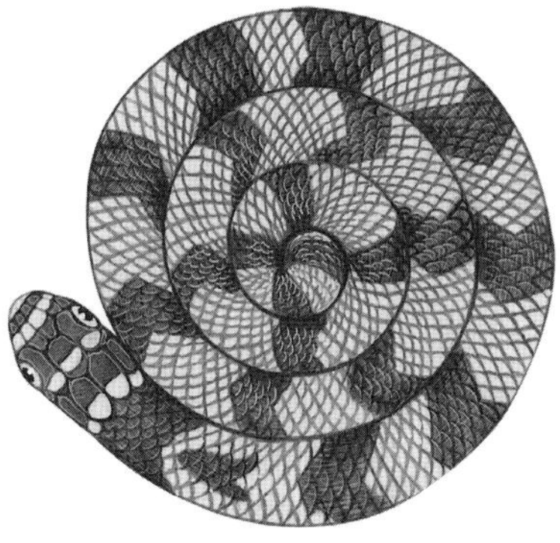

Lizard

King cobra

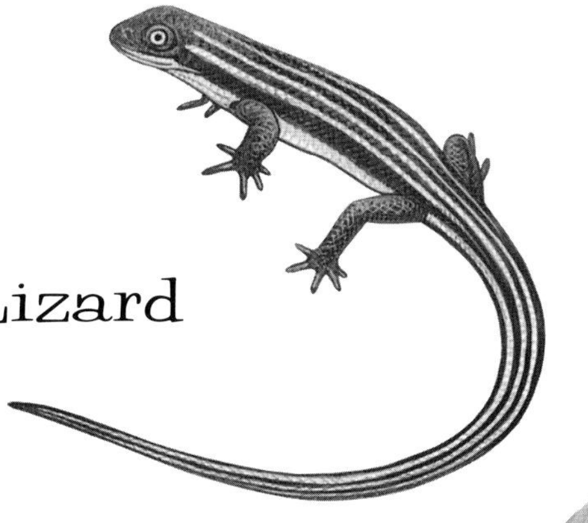

Gecko

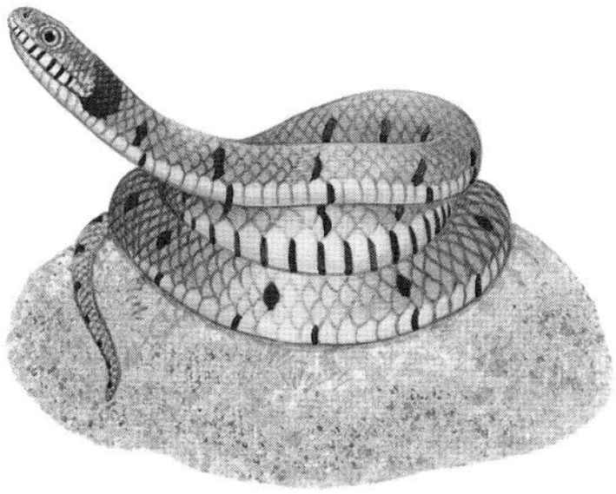

Tree snake

Chameleons

Interesting insects

There are more insects in the jungle than any other type of creature. Some are very strange-looking, which usually keeps them from being eaten by other animals. Can you see Bethany Bug using the eye spots on her back wings to frighten off the toucan? Use your stickers to add five more insects to the picture. What do you think the insect below is trying to look like?

Stick mantis

★ Creepy-crawlies!

Here are some of the strange insects and other creepy-crawlies that you might find in the jungle. Some might be hard to spot, but they're easy to hear! The male cicada likes to sing to the female and the cricket makes a noise by rubbing its wings together! Find the right stickers to fill in the pictures. Which one do you think is the strangest-looking bug?

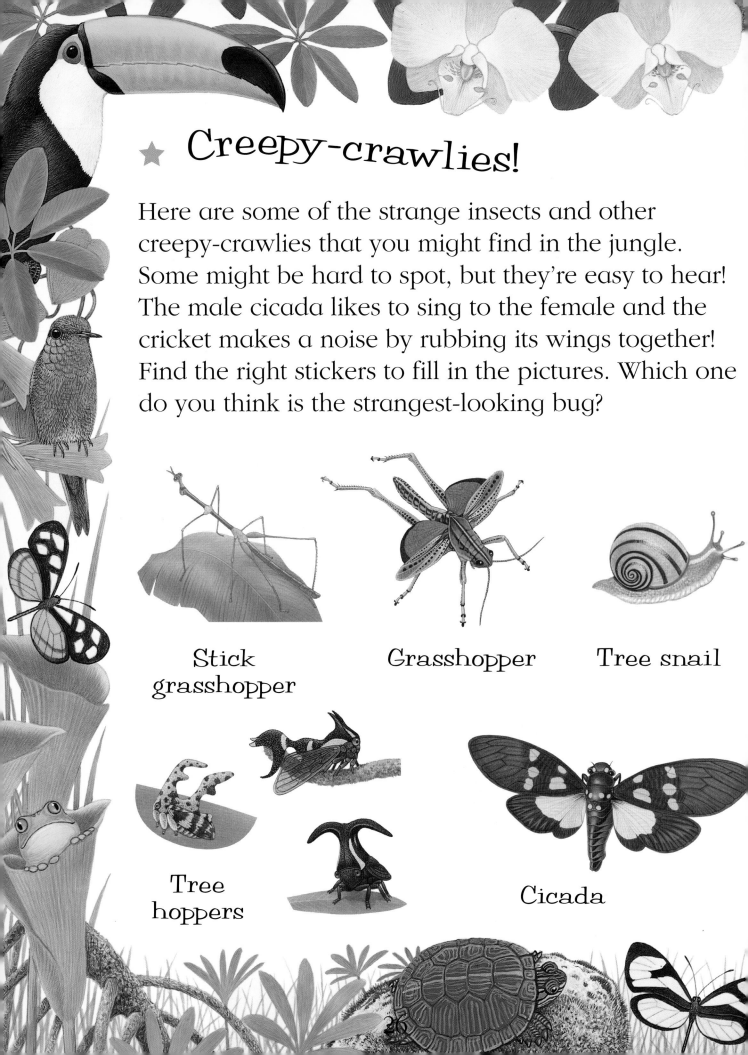

Stick grasshopper

Grasshopper

Tree snail

Tree hoppers

Cicada

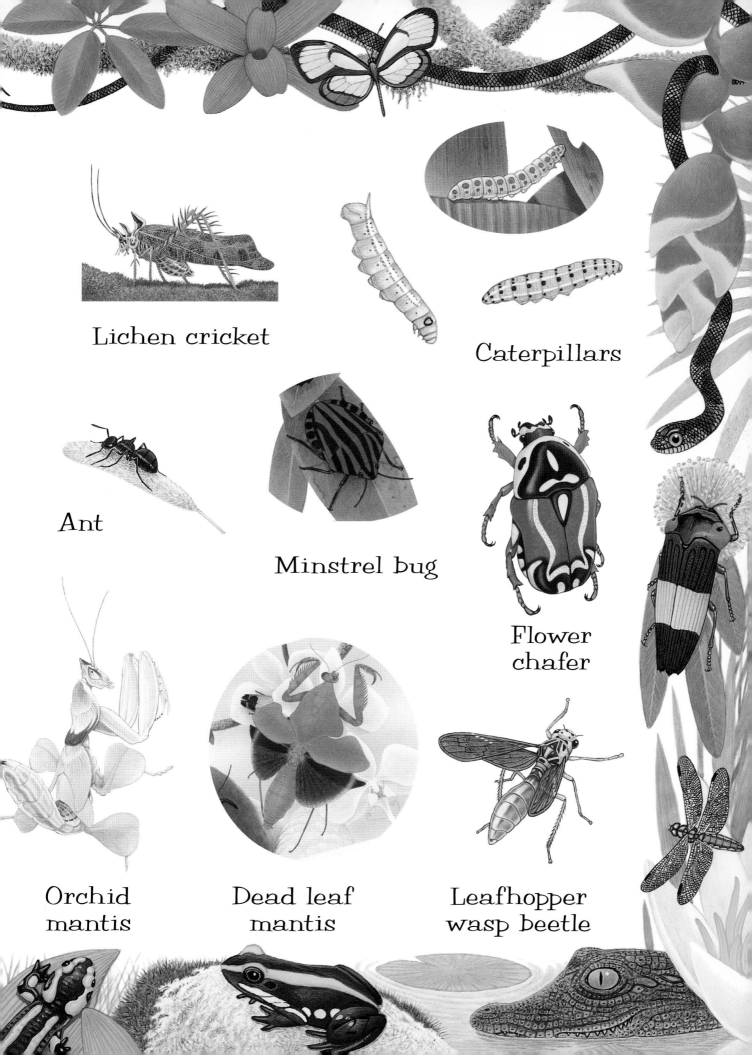

Lichen cricket

Caterpillars

Ant

Minstrel bug

Flower
chafer

Orchid
mantis

Dead leaf
mantis

Leafhopper
wasp beetle

★ Beetles and butterflies

Some of the most colorful jungle insects are the beetles and butterflies. Butterflies that live in the jungle may be much bigger than those you see in your garden—some are as big as your hand. And many beetles look like shiny jewels—some are even called jewel beetles, as they are so beautiful. Use your stickers to fill in these pictures of jungle beetles and butterflies. Then turn the page and make your own picture of insects in the jungle.

Jewel beetles

Stag beetle

Dung beetle

Hairy jewel beetle

Golden scarab

Birdwing
butterfly

Atlas
moth

Eyed moth

Peacock
butterfly

Tailed
birdwing

Glasswing
butterfly

Monteverde
butterfly

Agrias
butterfly

Ulysses
butterfly

29

Jungle plants

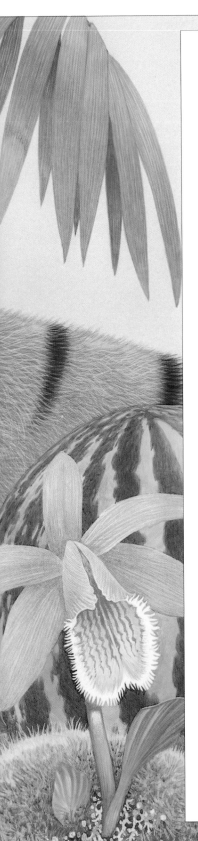

Plants are the most important part of life in the jungle, providing shelter and food for the creatures that live there. From towering trees to beautiful flowers, Tavi loves all the plants, but her favorites are orchids, like the ones shown here. Count how many she's found, then use your stickers to fill in the plants below.

This pitcher plant is a trap for bugs!

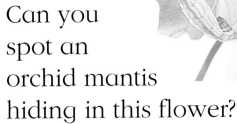

Can you spot an orchid mantis hiding in this flower?

Animal friends

Tavi has lost her friend Ollie Ocelot.
Use your sticker to add him to the scene.
How many of Tavi's other animal friends
can you see? Find out their names on the
next page, then add a sticker of a
mouse to complete the picture.

★ All kinds of animals

Here are some of Tavi Tiger's animal friends. Most of them live among the trees or on the jungle floor, but some of them, like the jaguar, are good swimmers, too. The cassowary is one of the few birds that you might find living on the jungle floor and for one very good reason—it cannot fly! Find the right stickers to fill in these pictures of Tavi's animal friends, then turn the page and make your own scene of life on the jungle floor.

Giant anteater

Long-eared bat

Mongoose

Cassowary

Ocelot

Golden lion
tamarin

Tree pangolin

Jaguar

Peccary

Tapir

Okapi

Capybara

All sorts of creatures live in or by the jungle river. Emma Egret stalks the shallows looking for fish, and the jaguar stops by for a drink. Use your stickers to add a hippopotamus, an ibis, and a dragonfly to the picture.

Frogs and their friends

Because of the warm, damp weather in the jungle, Frida Frog likes to live here. Some of Frida's friends live in the trees, while others live nearer the water. Some frogs are green and brown, so they can hide among the leaves and grasses. Other frogs, like Frida herself, are brightly colored. They are not scared of being noticed, since their bright colors are a warning that they are poisonous!

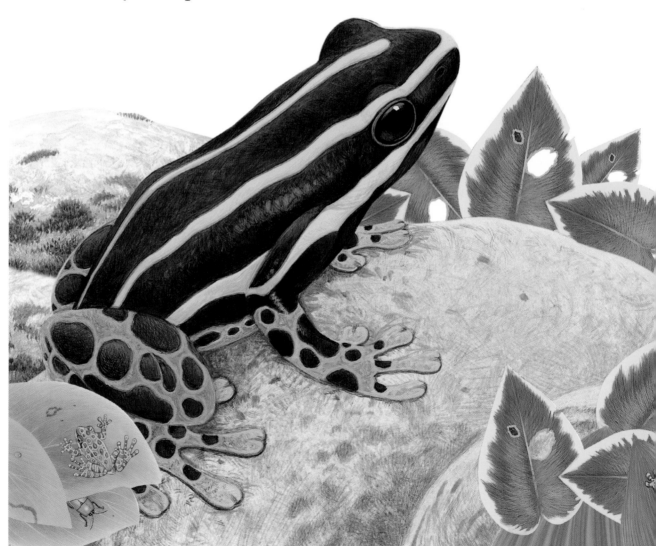

Frogs are part of a family of animals called amphibians, living on land and in the water. Match the stickers from your sticker sheet to Frida Frog's amphibian friends below.

Amazon
poison frog

Tree frogs

Newts

Salamander

★ Water creatures

Emma Egret has lots of friends who live in or by the jungle river. Some of them can't be seen because they like living underwater, like piranhas or swordfish. The huge hippopotamus likes to wallow in the shallow water, keeping his skin cool and wet. Find the right stickers for these special water creatures. Then turn the page and use your stickers to make a lively scene of the jungle, featuring some of the friends you have met!

Hippopotamus

Amazon river dolphin

Swordfish

Gavial

Black piranha

Dragonfly

Emma Egret

Glossy ibis

Crocodiles

The gavial is a close cousin of the crocodile. You can tell them apart because the gavial's snout is longer and thinner than the crocodile's.

How to use your stickers

Look for the page numbers on the sticker sheets to help you find the right stickers for the different activities in this book. Peel each one carefully from its backing sheet and use it to fill in the shapes or add to the scenes.

You can also use your stickers to record the animals you see in real life. Look for the creatures in this book if you are at the zoo, then fill in their sticker shapes as you see them. Some animals are easier to find than others. Some may not live where you do, so look for them when you travel.

Enjoy your adventure through the amazing jungle world!

Add to scene on pages 6–7

Pages 8–9

More stickers for pages 8–9

Pages 10–11

Pages 12–13

Pages 14–15

Pages 18–19

Pages 20–21

Pages 22–23

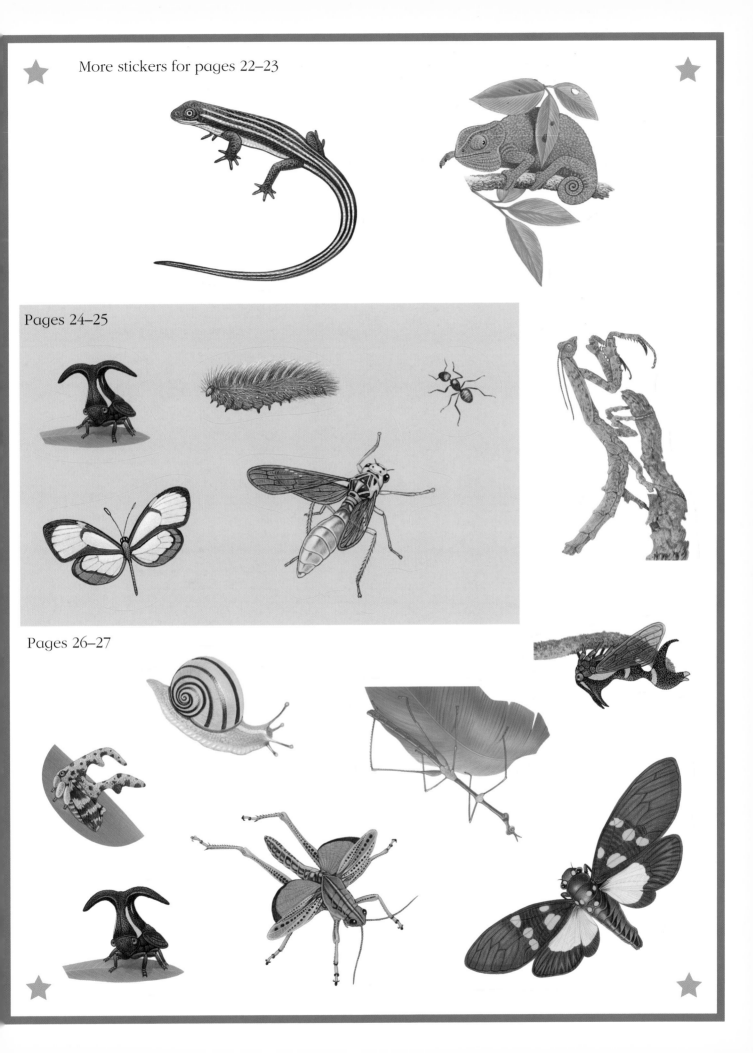

More stickers for pages 22–23

Pages 24–25

Pages 26–27

More stickers for pages 26–27

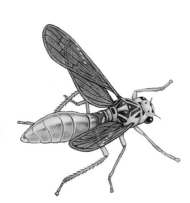

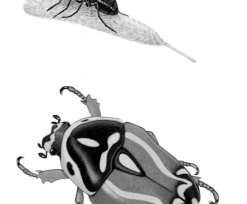

Pages 28–29

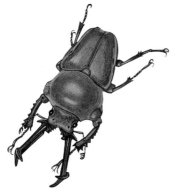

Pages 32–33

Add to scene on pages 34–35

Pages 36–37

Add to scene on pages 38–39

Add to scene on pages 40–41

Pages 42–43

Add to scene on pages 46–47